The Web

Alison Hawes • Jon Stuart

Bugtastic

Contents

OXFORD
UNIVERSITY PRESS

Macro Marvel
(billionaire inventor)

Welcome to Micro World!

Macro Marvel invented Micro World –
a micro-sized theme park where you have
to shrink to get in.

A computer called **CODE** controls
Micro World and all the robots inside –
MITEs and BITEs.

A MITE

A BITE

Disaster strikes!

CODE goes wrong on opening day.
CODE wants to shrink the world.

Macro Marvel is trapped inside the park …

Enter Team X!

Four micro agents – *Max, Cat, Ant* and *Tiger* – are sent to rescue Macro Marvel and defeat CODE.

Mini Marvel joins Team X.

Mini Marvel
(Macro's daughter)

Together they have to:

- Defeat the BITES
- Collect the CODE keys
- Rescue Macro Marvel
- Stop CODE
- Save the world!

CODE key

Look at the map on page 4. You are in the Bugtastic zone.

3

Before you read

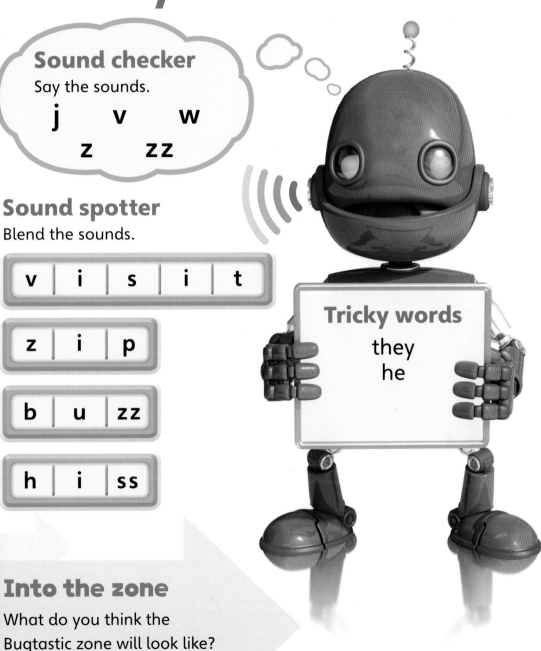

Sound checker
Say the sounds.

j   v   w

z   zz

Sound spotter
Blend the sounds.

| v | i | s | i | t |

| z | i | p |

| b | u | zz |

| h | i | ss |

Tricky words
they
he

Into the zone
What do you think the
Bugtastic zone will look like?

Jump On!

Max, Cat, Ant and Tiger visit the bugs.

Mini visits the bugs as well.

They jump on the Big Bug and off they go!
They zip past lots of bugs.

zip!

Ant has a job.
He will snap the bugs.
Snap!
Is it the BITE?

I buzz!

I hiss!

I jump!

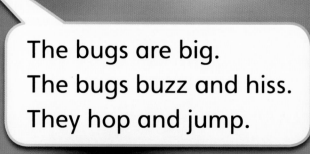

The bugs are big.
The bugs buzz and hiss.
They hop and jump.

Now you have read ...
Jump On!

Text checker
What did Ant take pictures of?

Snap!

MITE fun
Look back at the story.
What do bugs do?

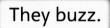 They buzz.

 They hiss.

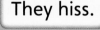 They jump.

Did you spot me?

Before you read

Sound checker

Say the sounds.

j   v   w

z   zz

Sound spotter

Blend the sounds.

| v | a | s | t |

| w | e | b |

| j | u | s | t |

| w | e | ll |

Tricky words

are
they
she
he

Into the zone

Why do Team X and Mini
need the CODE key?

The Big Bug

Team X and Mini are on the Big Bug ride.
They must get to the BITE.
They must get the CODE key.

On the visit they see lots of bugs.

The Big Bug ride has to stop.
A vast web is on the track!

Help!

Cat sees a big bug.
She jumps and runs off.

Max tells Cat to stop.

Stop!

Cat will not stop.
She just runs and runs.

Max looks for Cat.

The bug jumps at Cat.

Then Max sees Cat.

Zip! Zap!
He stops the bug.

Cat runs.
She runs fast.

Max runs fast as well.
They get back to the Big Bug ride.

Now you have read ...
The Big Bug

Text checker
What was Cat thinking?

MITE fun
Look back at the story.
Can you retell the story using
the pictures?